ELIMINATING POVERTY THROUGH INVESTMENT

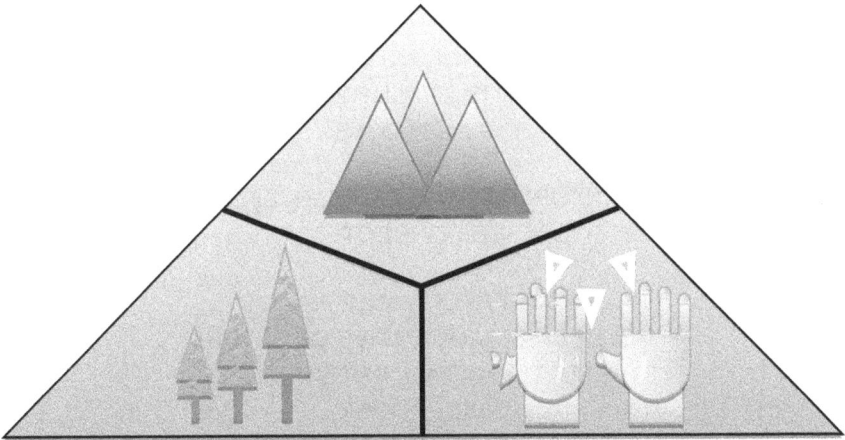

By: Forest Cherrytree

Copyright © 2018
Published by:
Forest Cherrytree
Oshkosh, WI, 54901, USA

ISBN: 978-1-949726-00-8

RISK DISCLAIMER

EVERYTHING PRESENTED IS FOR
INFORMATIONAL, EDUCATIONAL, OR
PURPOSES THAT HAVE NO LEGAL
LIABILITIES.

NO PART OF THIS WORK SHOULD BE
INTERPRETED AS FINANCIAL ADVICE
OR PERSONAL FINANCIAL ADVICE.

THE AUTHOR NOR ANYONE
MENTIONED IS AT ALL RESPONSIBLE
FOR ANY LOSSES.

NO INFORMATION IS GUARANTEED TO
BE CORRECT.

PAST PERFORMANCE IS NOT
NECESSARILY INDICATIVE OF FUTURE
RESULTS, AND ALL INVESTMENTS
INVOLVE RISK.

EVERYTHING SHOULD BE
INDEPENDENTLY VERIFIED.

PEOPLE'S NAMES USED ONLY TO
GIVE CREDIT, SHOW RESPECT, OR
PARODY, OR THEIR IDEAS MAY BE
MISUNDERSTOOD; THAT IS NOT TO
SAY THEY ENDORSE ANY IDEAS IN
THIS WORK.

EACH INDIVIDUAL IS SOLELY
RESPONSIBLE FOR THEIR
INVESTMENT AND TRADING
DECISIONS.

JUST ONE QUESTION

What would you choose between these two?

A) At least $25,000 yearly payout per person on Earth inflation adjusted in 900 years.

B) $1000 immediately split among everyone on Earth.

That is less than a penny per person.

ANSWER

If you chose B, then you probably don't have time to read this book and need money in the short term.

I suggest not wasting your time on this book!

If you chose A, then you may continue.

SUMMARY

$1,000 can eventually eliminate poverty by safely growing wealth, paying out the correct ratio of growth, and providing an incentive for population stability.

CONTENTS

CURRENT SITUATION

First, we must see the
current situation and trends,
then we can improve them.

!??

First, see what you think independently, then I will share my finding, and you can take anything that you find useful.

Estimate the following:

1) Is the world improving or getting worse for the average person versus 200 years ago and before that?

2) What about income for most people in the US for the last 40 years?

Life has been improving, for people on average, through technological throughout history, especially during the last 200 years.

To demonstrate before 1800, four of six children would die before maturity. [i]

Thus, women had to have at least six children on average to keep the species going.

Now, most people survive to adulthood.

Another example, in 1900 over 30% of the US population were farmers out of necessity to provide food, so people did not starve.

Presently, less than 2% of the population are farmers. [ii]

This efficiency improvement shows the extent to which

farmers improved technology to provide food for billions of people.

That means, farmers innovated to grow more food, versus 100 years ago, with fewer people in absolute and relative terms.

Therefore, the overall situation is significantly better than 200 years ago.

That was overall, now for some things that need to improve faster, such as the total death rate improved for the last 50 years, yet not necessarily at a historic minimum, therefore ought to improve faster. [iii]

In specific for America, the situation does not feel so optimistic because for the last 40 years 60% of the US population's income barely improved. [iv]

Income stagnated when compared to housing prices.

This stagnation is an outrage!

Some people have given up hope on improving themselves and things for everyone.

Someone ought to fix that 40-year trend.

Plans to improve that come later.

For now, onto population.

A common belief is that if we progress, then people will have more children nullifying improvement in individual lives.

I respectfully disagree.

If someone takes the time to consider the present situation and trends and makes plans to improve, then things can improve.

To greatly increase inflation adjusted wealth, one must improve efficiency or stability.

For example, food because food is easy to visualize.

For farmers to make as much improvement as they did in the last 100 years, they would have to improve food at least ten times…

…improve in yearly abundance, quality, nutritional value, or some combination.

Some other possibilities include improving housing, energy, or creating technology.

By investing in the people and companies that may create that kind of value through innovation, one has a high probability of sharing some of the profit in a functioning market. [v]

Investing and growing wealth to be covered in the following section.

GROWING WEALTH

A simple investing strategy is suggested to provide a high probability of stable growth.

!??

Test your skills.

Find:

1) Can you find an investing strategy that would have survived and grown wealth in past markets since the creation of stocks 2,000 years ago?

2) What is the long-term risk and reward compared to most investors in the market index?

Global wealth can be increased through investment, so that future generations may live better than present.

Unfortunately, safely increasing wealth is challenging.

Three generations of people lose most of the wealth from ancestors, in part due to spending or donating a slightly excessive amount.

This is demonstrated by the wealthiest families in the US 100 years ago that had over $300 billion adjusted for inflation.

Less than 10% of the initial value remains.

That wealth loss is not their fault – it is simply a common trend.

Like how inflation slowly reduces the value of a US dollar to a small fraction of the long-term value.

Another example is seen in times of economic downturn when companies must fire employees to survive.

Then economic recessions and depressions make finding a job difficult for most index investors.

So, they must sell their stock holdings at any price to pay for food and shelter for self and family.

The average person cannot handle an 85% loss, as shown by the increased suicide rate during the great depression after 1929. [vi]

Careful planning can improve the situation.

Investing is analogous to medicine.

When a doctor recommends something to a patient, they want these things:

A) Efficiency, being the best care for the patient at the lowest price in the fastest time.

B) Stability, meaning avoiding large risks.

C) Improvement, as in becoming better instead of worse.

That is the same for investing, in general, increase wealth, avoid large losses like 50% to 85%, and avoid financial death which is 100% loss over the extremely long term.

The principals used in determining an investment strategy follows:

1) Absolute return, meaning the gain or loss in purchasing value.

2) Alpha, the return compared to the benchmark index.

3) Downside Deviation, the negative side of standard deviation. (Some investors use somewhat related things like beta or volatility.)

4) Maximum Drawdown, the percentage loss from crest to trough.

5) Extremely Long-Term Maximum Risk, one must check if the use of a strategy resulted in bankruptcy during past markets since the creation of stocks 2,000 years ago.

Those are the general principles

To safely grow we must consider assets that grow and things that stay safe during complete financial meltdowns.

Assets that grow include stocks and bonds.

However, repeatedly beating the stock market is more difficult than winning at the Olympics. [vii]

Fortunately, to eliminate poverty, we do not have to beat the market; instead we must prioritize safe growth.

When stocks are mentioned the intended meaning is an index of the entire market or an index largest companies; both of those will be similar because naturally the S&P 500 takes up about 75% of the market. [viii]

Stocks and bonds flourish during different parts of productivity and debt cycles, which Ray Dalio explains well in the short video called *How The Economic Machine Works.* [ix]

Stocks were invented about 2,000 years ago during the Roman Republic, and were called publicani according to Dr. Ziemba. [x]

Those stocks became worthless when the Republic fell, and the Roman Empire rose.

A strategy that would have survived in past markets since the creation of stocks gives the highest probability of surviving long into the future.

Most of the population is unable to predict or prepare for catastrophes.

Unpredictable events which have a large impact are known as *Black Swans* according to Nassim Taleb. [xi]

Since predicting a Black Swan is improbable, we should plan a simple mix of assets and rebalance yearly.

However, stocks and bonds have become completely worthless during a catastrophe when a country collapses or nationalizes all private property and profits.

The safest possibility combines growth assets with safe assets.

Safe assets are commodities.

People consume commodities for energy, like food for humans, oil for machines, or gold to store value.

Not to say that commodities will not lose value or be substituted, but these survive a complete financial collapse.

A combination of growth and safety, if properly balanced, creates more safety than holding any safety or growth index.

Further, the assets should be stored in as many locations as needed to minimize risk.

Locations must be safe and unrelated.

Fifteen locations would be ideal; five locations are realistic for a successful corporation; only one location is possible for the average person.

We want a strategy that will grow at least as fast as the median person investing in the stock index, stayed safe for the last 100 years, and would have survived the past markets of the last 2,000 years.

The median index investor receives around half the average annual return of the index; this concept is known as behavior adjusted return. [xii]

We set our goals as follows.

A) At least ½ of the stock markets average annual growth, so about 5% annual growth before inflation or 3.5% after inflation.

B) Under 1/3 of the stock markets risk for the last 100 years.

C) A strategy that could have survived in past markets since the invention of stocks 2,000 years ago.

In 1970, Harry Browne introduced the first strategy that would have survived past markets of the last 2,000 years and accomplish most of the other goals. [xiii]

In 2014, Ray Dalio shared the "All Seasons" strategy with everyone during an Interview with Tony Robbins. [xiv]

The All Seasons strategy meets our goals, yet there are issues for the average person. [xv]

First, publicly available data only goes back to 2006 on a broad commodities basket including oil, natural gas, soy, wheat, coffee, and others.

Second, storing many commodities costs too much for the average person.

Therefore, we select only gold for commodities, due to current information and markets.

Combining Harry Brown and Ray Dalio's portfolios satisfies our goal.

The following is Forest's 901 Year Strategy.

Rebalanced yearly by the controller of the fund,

- 35% Stocks

- 35% Long-term bonds

- 15% Intermediate bonds

- 15% Gold

Strategy simplified with Electronically Traded Funds (ETFs).[xvi]

Below are examples of easy ways to invest in those assets

- 35% Stocks represented by the Vanguard Total Stock Market ETF searchable by the symbol VTI.

- 35% Long-term Bonds represented by iShares Barclay's 20+ Year Treasury Bond ETF searchable by the symbol TLT.

- 15% Intermediate Bonds represented by iShares

Barclay's 7-10 Year Treasury Bond Fund searchable by the symbol IEF.

- 15% Gold represented by iShares Gold Trust which holds gold bars in vaults around the world searchable by the symbol IAU.

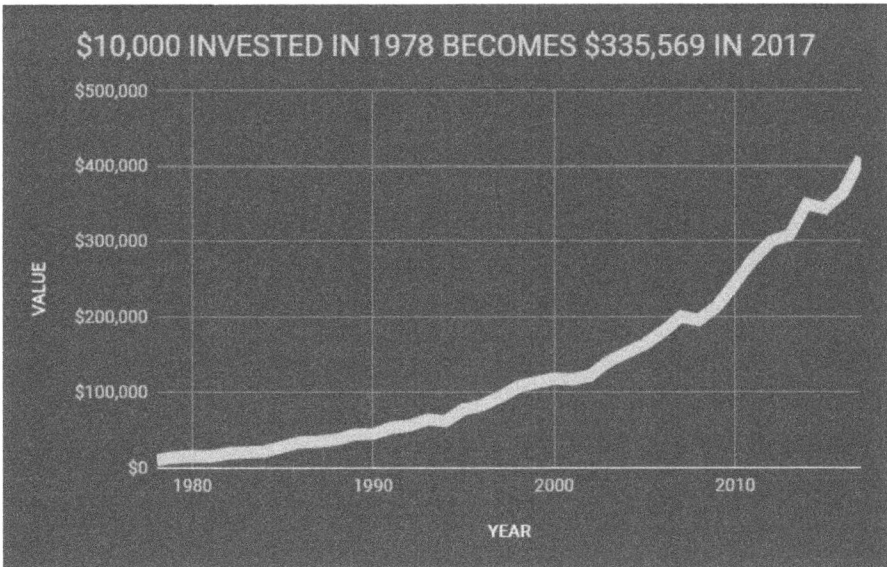

$10,000 INVESTED IN 1978 BECOMES $335,569 IN 2017

Figure 1.

Forest's 901 Year Strategy back tested.

$10,000 initially invested in 1978 would have grown to $410,000 in 2017.

The compounded annual growth rate from 1978 to 2017 was 9.73%.

After 0.5% fees that shrinks to 9.18% because of the damage caused by that on low or negative growth years.

Starting with $10,000 in 1978 would have grown to $410,000 in 2017.

Anyone can test for themselves on *portfolio visualizer*. [xvii]

Inflation should be considered to comprehend the purchasing value.

Inflation is estimated higher at 3.67% a year from 1978 to 2017.

That yields 5.5% growth after inflation and fees.

The maximum drawdown would be 85% during complete financial collapses or nationalization.

Every financial system completely collapsed at least once during the last 2,000 years. [xviii]

A collapse is tragic, which is why we need the gold – to survive, unlike the local currency and markets.

If properly secured, then the gold could be kept safe.

For more common depressions and recessions, this strategy fared much better.

During the great depression from 1929 to 1932, stocks lost over

85% of their value, while gold significantly increased in value.

Thus, keeping the loss below 1/3 of the total value.

More recently during the 2008 financial crisis, the maximum drawdown was under 15% and the worst year was under a 5% loss.

We considered the worst-case scenarios that are possible to survive.

We have a safe growth strategy.

The expected growth rate is 5.5%.

Next, we need to determine the optimum amount of payout each year.

SHARING RESOURCES

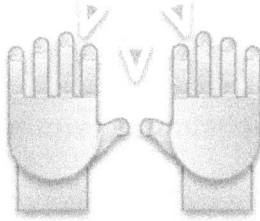

Sharing too little fails to improve things during a normal lifetime.

Sharing too much becomes unsustainable and leaves everyone disappointed in the long term.

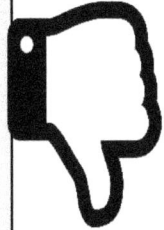

The proper ratio to share can be mathematically determined to maximize payout.

!??

This question is extremely challenging.

Mathematically determine:

1) The most efficient percentage of total wealth to share for 100 years, using the previous growth rate of 5.5%, answer in the percentage of profit and percentage of total value.

By safely growing resources an increasing amount can be shared each year.

Many people think that others don't want to help others.

I disagree.

A lot of people do want to share wealth because people in the US donated $390 billion to charitable causes in 2017.[xix]

Finding an effective payout percentage presents a challenge.

Paying out too much creates false hope only to disappoint people when you or the fund inevitably goes bankrupt.

If too little is paid out, then people can't enjoy enough of the reward during their lives.

Ed Thorp discovered that the efficient payout percentage of an account with 10% growth is 2%. [xx]

First, we need to convert that to a general rule based on profit.

The payout, in general, should be 20% of average net profit.

We have a 5.5% growth rate.

For a stable payout, that is 1.1% of the total value paid out each year.

The following graph visually demonstrates that a yearly payout of 20% of net profit pays out the maximum amount over an average lifetime.

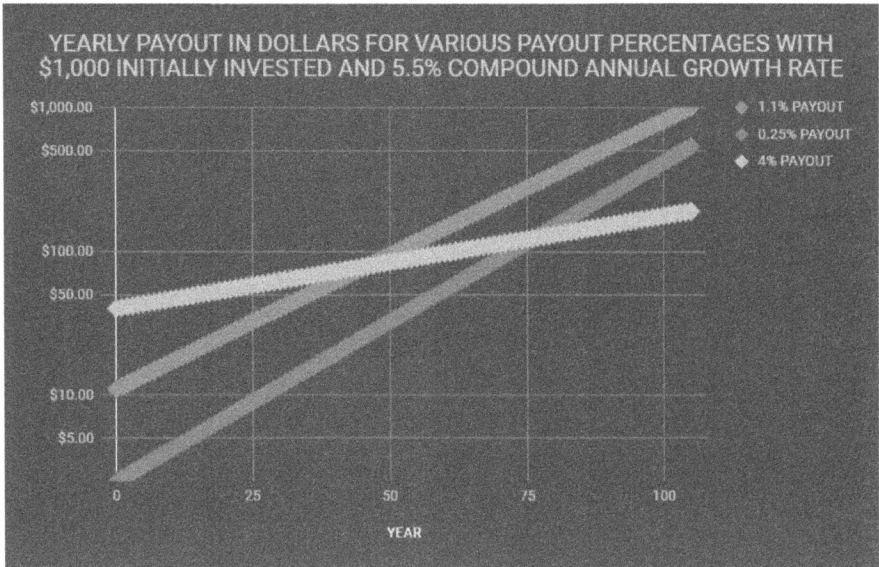

YEARLY PAYOUT IN DOLLARS FOR VARIOUS PAYOUT PERCENTAGES WITH $1,000 INITIALLY INVESTED AND 5.5% COMPOUND ANNUAL GROWTH RATE

Figure 2.

1.1% annual payout maximizes payout over 105 years.

Payouts percentages listed in order of final value and on a logarithmic scale for easy viewing.

In 105 years, the yearly payout is higher than the initial amount invested.

For comparison, an irresponsible payout ratio like 6% leads to

decline, as shown in the following
graph.

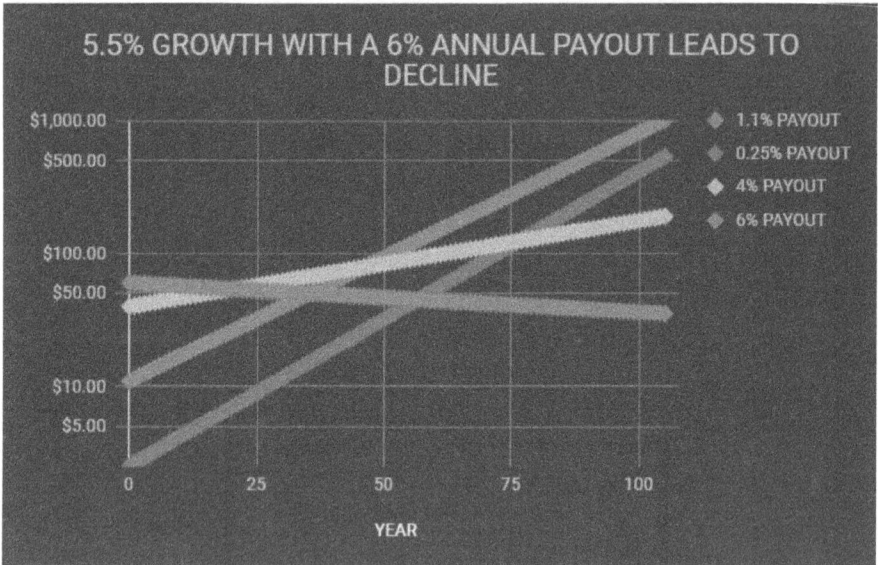

5.5% GROWTH WITH A 6% ANNUAL PAYOUT LEADS TO DECLINE

Figure 3.

A 6% payout decreases in
payout each year.

This demonstrates wasted
potential.

The previous graphs show that
unplanned payout will lead to
depletion while efficient payout
will lead to many times the
original value paid out.

Combining precise payout with growth creates an increasing yearly payout.

$1,000 initial investment yields a small payout the first year, yearly payout equal to the initial investment after 105 years, and $744 quadrillion yearly payout after 900 years.

INITIAL INVESTMENT AND PAYOUT

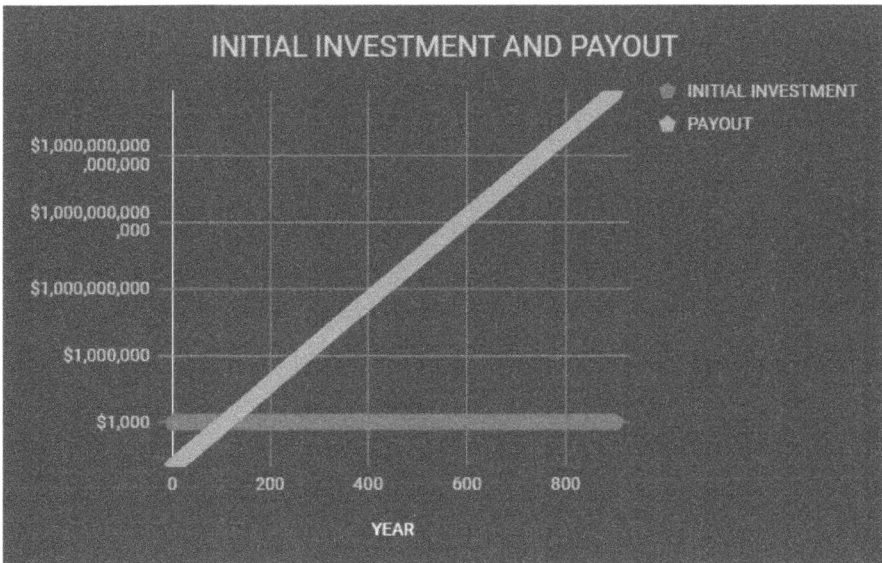

Legend:
- INITIAL INVESTMENT
- PAYOUT

Y-axis values:
- $1,000,000,000,000,000
- $1,000,000,000,000
- $1,000,000,000
- $1,000,000
- $1,000

X-axis (YEAR): 0, 200, 400, 600, 800

Figure 4.

$1,000 grown at 4.4% after all inflation and fees with a 1.1% yearly payout will payout annually $744 quadrillion after 900 years.

If the population stabilizes, then that payout will lift everyone out of absolute poverty.

STABILIZING POPULATION

Stabilize the population
through financial incentives.

!??

Research and find:

1) What is the most
   important factor in
   stabilizing population?

2) How to stabilize the
   population without
   biological warfare,
   nukes, terminators, or
   other harmful force?

The plan for eliminating poverty through growing and sharing resources only works if the population stabilizes.

Otherwise, this plan may cause unstable population growth.

According to professor Hans Rosling, the most important factor in stabilizing population across cultures and religions is a reasonable certainty for the family that two children will survive to maturity. [xxi]

If the children survive, that increases the parent survival chances in old age because their children are the only ones who will be able to provide for them in extremely low resource areas where people live on less than $1 a day.

Furthermore, people want to continue their genetic code.

Contrary to popular belief, the most common family size on Earth is two parents and two children.

Before around 200 years ago, life on Earth was so difficult and deadly that four of six people would die before adulthood.

Thus, nature required women to have six children on average to continue our species.

Thanks to our ancestors for improving medicine and technology, we can survive more comfortably.

Since 1800, the population on Earth boomed to 7.6 billion today and will hopefully stabilize at 12 billion people through the following proposal.

To get to 12 billion most of that is from demographics stabilizing with each couple having 2 kids.

As previously mentioned the largest risk factor is uncertainty if their children will survive.

Then, many families have six children for a good chance that two will survive like in Niger, Angola, and Mali.[xxii]

Eventually, this plan will provide enough wealth to bring everyone out of extreme poverty like in countries where people must have many children for a high probability that two will survive.

However, the plan must financially incentivize stable population to avoid people using funds to have too many kids and overpopulate.

Also considering some countries, like Germany and Japan where the population is at risk of declining because people are not having enough kids.

Not to say that someone must have kids, only to incentivize healthy families.

Also, families could have more than two kids but must provide the resources themselves.

Population to be stabilized by a bonus factor in payout per individual.

Bonus pays out more for people with one or two kids to help families provide for their children, and reduced payout for people with more than two children to avoid overpopulation.

The bonus and equation for payout follows.

0 kids = 1x

1 kid = 1.25x

2 kids = 1.35x

3 kids = 0.75x

4 kids = 0.375x...

...and continuing to half.

Payout for individual =

$$\left(\frac{Total\ Payout}{Number\ Of\ People}\right) *$$

$$\left(\frac{(1\ +\ bonus)}{(1\ +\ average\ bonus)}\right)$$

That equation is the most effective to stabilize population presently available because living beyond absolute poverty provides the maximum certainty that children will live to adulthood.

By combining stable population at 12 billion with the previously mentioned strategy for growing and sharing resources, then current levels of poverty on Earth will be eliminated.

The following graph shows the yearly payout per person for 12 billion people if you or I invest $1,000.

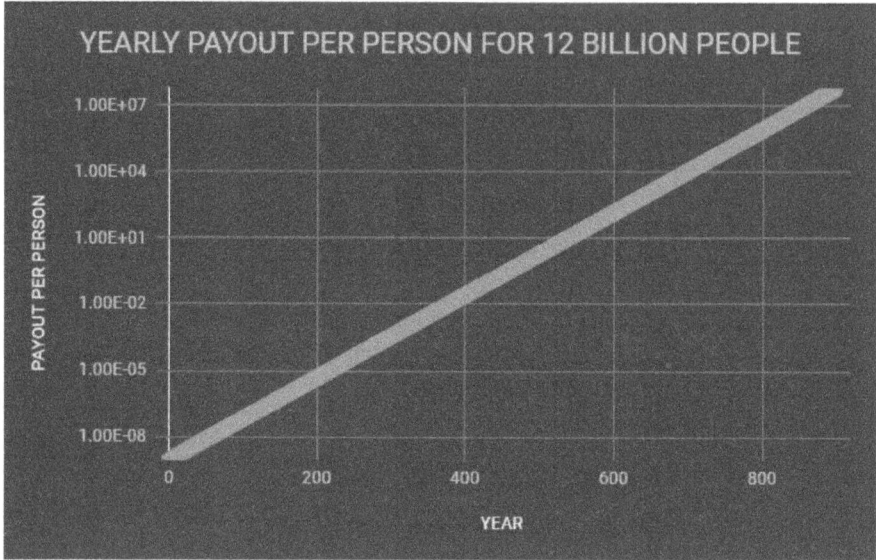

YEARLY PAYOUT PER PERSON FOR 12 BILLION PEOPLE

Figure 5.

Our plan will yield $62 million yearly per person for 12 billion people in 900 years.

That is from an initial investment of $1,000.

For clarification on the chart, note the bottom three lines on the vertical axis have a negative exponent meaning they are a small fraction of one dollar.

We can see the top line of the chart reads 1.00E+07.

This means $1*10^7$, which is 10,000,000.

So, the top line, is ten million dollars per year.

The graph shows us exceeding that.

The yearly payout is $62 million inflation adjusted per person on Earth in 900 years...

...many times $25,000 per family per year, as the US government defines the poverty threshold in the US. [xxiii]

This plan expects to significantly outperform the initial goal of eliminating poverty because nothing ever goes as planned.

A high goal of ten million per person per year allows a margin of error for unforeseen set-backs or difficulties.

Perhaps the initial goal to eliminate poverty seems too slow.

Well, this plan can be sped up by investing more initially.

Either way, this maximizes efficiently eliminating poverty.

Each factor of 1,000 reduces poverty elimination time by about 160 years.

- An initial investment of $1,000 eliminates poverty in 900 years.

- $1 million takes 740 years.

- $1 billion takes 580 years to get there.

- $1 trillion requires 420 years.

If we reach the goal of eliminating absolute poverty, then this plan will continue financially improving life for everyone.

CONCLUSION

Combining growth, payout, and population make eliminating poverty possible.

The overall goal is to eliminate poverty efficiently.

Three key details are growing wealth, sharing resources, and stabilizing population.

Forest's 901 Year Strategy is selected to grow wealth.

Rebalanced yearly by the controller of the fund,

- 35% Stocks

- 35% Long-term bonds

- 15% Intermediate bonds

- 15% Gold

The expected growth rate is 5.5% after inflation and fees.

To payout the maximum amount over time, we adapt Ed Thorp's ratio to 20% of average net profit on 5.5% growth.

This plan's payout ratio is 1.1% of the total value annual payout distributed between everyone.

Population to be stabilized at 12 billion incentivizing stability and reducing payout for people overpopulating.

The extra payout for people with one or two kids, less payout for people with three or more kids.

Combining those concepts one person could invest $1,000 and it would eliminate poverty for everyone in 900 years.

The yearly payout would be $62 million per person for 12 billion people.

Yearly payout grows safely and efficiently because we precisely planned the payout ratios.

We planned for multiple complete financial collapses, to plan for bad economic conditions.

However, if the economy performs well, or we increase initial investment, then we will eliminate poverty quicker.

END

P.S.

Additional details.

-EXAMPLE

-RESEARCH
 OPPORTUNITIES

-RISKS

-THANKS

-REFERENCES

EXAMPLE

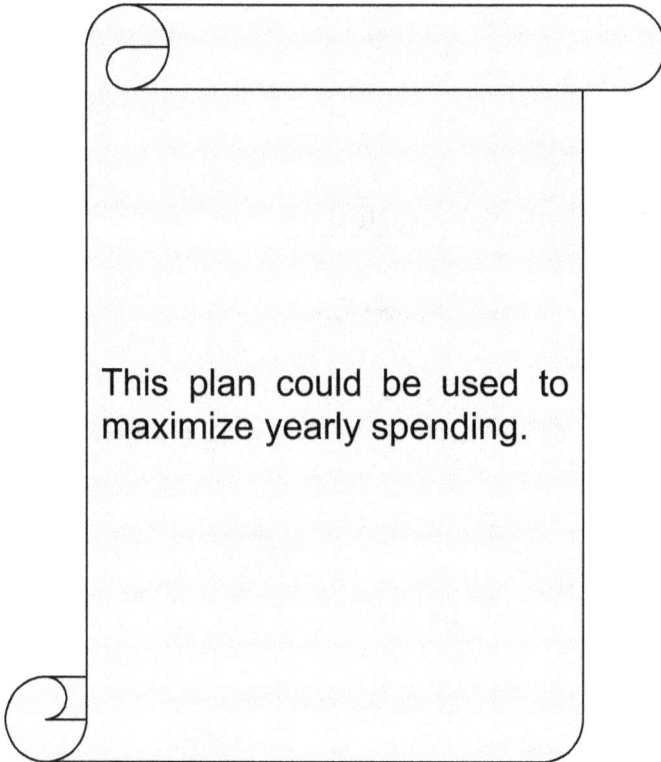

This plan could be used to maximize yearly spending.

To maximize personal spending over the long term, take out about 1.1% of the total yearly and grow the rest.

That is 1.1% per 5.5% net average annual growth.

That is the optimum amount to use yearly.

Historically, many people think their culture and technology is close to perfect, that is as advanced as possible.

This is clearly incorrect and there are many ways to improve, but improvement is very challenging.

1) Blockchain could be used to make the plan more transparent.

2) Someone could continue improve this plan to make it simpler and more effective.

3) Another could create strategies with similar goals or criteria.

4) Each section should be improved as new information becomes available.

   Maybe a new asset class like new technology will be defined and tested for the last 2,000 years.

   Or someone will compile a longer data history of commodities, stocks, and bonds.

5) Test this plan across as many countries markets as possible.

6) Add an optional auto opt-in or opt-out for each person doing an additional five minutes of work at 5 pm or selected time to improve life for people.

Then on average individual wealth is expected to increase faster because that was Masayoshi Son's plan to become one of the wealthiest people on Earth and improve technology.

He succeeded and quickly became the wealthiest man on Earth for a short time.

One could use Masayoshi's plan to improve at efficiency every day like an athlete.

For consideration, the bonus payout could be 50% paid out before, and 50% paid out after each person says on their honor that they worked 5 minutes a day or week on their selected purpose.

That should be researched and see if people have a stronger sense of purpose that way.

7) Country-specific funds should be established for a friendly competition to see which country is most generous.

50% paid out in country and 50% for everyone.

RISKS

Anything worth doing has risks.

The risks should be identified and considered along with the rewards.

Considering good outcomes and risks provides the best probability for things to turn out well when at the planning stage for improving something. [xxiv] [xxv] [xxvi] [xxvii]

Not saying to think negative or at all when warming up for something like batting in baseball, but useful for the planning phase.

We should consider the following risks when making a 900-year plan.

1) The risk of not improving is greatest because the sun will become a red giant and incinerate all life on Earth in billions of years.

   Therefore, we must improve our technology to survive.

```
┌─────────────────────────┐
│ Stay the same or get    │
│ worse                   │
│ -> eventually be        │
│ incinerated by the      │
│ sun.                    │
└─────────────────────────┘
┌──────────────────┐
│ To improve       │
│ technology?      │
└──────────────────┘
┌─────────────────────────┐
│ Technologically         │
│ improve                 │
│ -> best chance to       │
│ survive.                │
└─────────────────────────┘
```

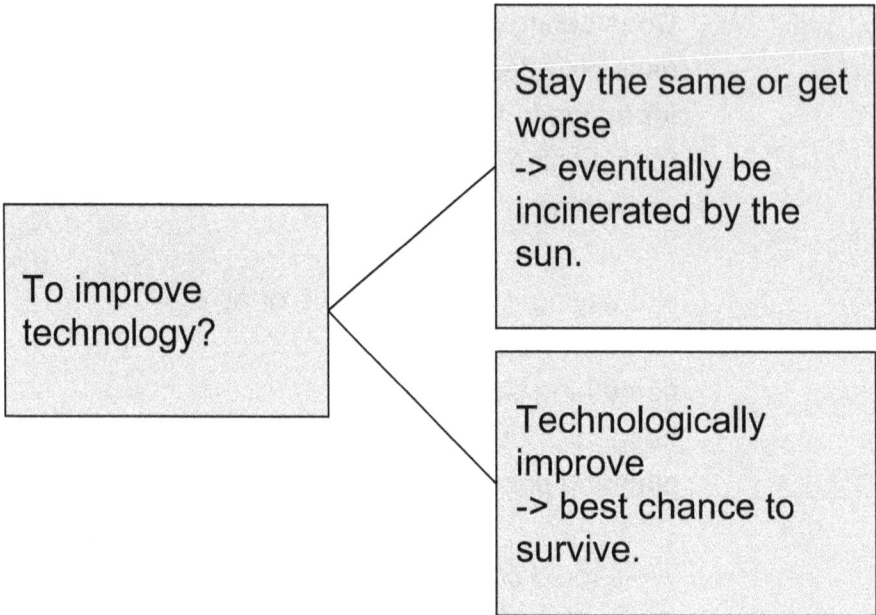

2) When improving technology, that makes destroying ourselves easier for everyone.

This is a present and alarming danger.

Hopefully, helping eliminate extreme poverty will reduce the threat of us destroying ourselves.

3) Theft, internal or external, could cause significant losses, individuals or funds must mitigate that risk like any business.

4) People may try to take advantage of the system or create fake accounts.

   Payout distribution must follow standard know your customer procedure as many businesses or charities.

5) Poverty traps show up in some welfare programs when something is provided only for people under a certain income.

   The trap exists when people would lose welfare thing if they earn any income.

   For example, why would someone take a job paying

$500 a month, welfare pays $1,000 a month!

In this case, taking the job would cause an income loss.

The best way to help people is treating them all as an equal and helping the same.

The aid or encouragement should be consistent and efficient to not become annoying by being around too much.

6) The fund controller must keep fees to a minimum, or else the fund may fail.

7) There are always set-backs and difficulties which are unpredictable and impossible to prepare for.

Still, best to use the plan
with the most potential,
most promising outcome,
and monitor progress.

THANKS

Thanks to the following.

Harry Browne and Ray Dalio created a way to safely grow resources and survive even the worst catastrophes which are possible to survive.

William Ziemba, Kory Hoang, Cameron Skinner, John Connor, Claude Shannon, Riley Gilbertson, and John Kelly taught me scenario modelling through communication or information.

Ed Thorp found a way to payout an efficiently increasing amount every year.

Dillon Kuester for sharing *Chat With Traders* and Hans Rosling's YouTube videos; and Aaron Fifield for making chat with traders.

Hans Rosling and his son Ola Rosling researched and presented population statistics in a way that anyone could understand the most important factors.

My friends and family told me the previous 42 drafts were too long and wordy, now publishing that they got bored of telling me that or this version is good enough.

This writing style comes from Neil Strauss and Dr. Suhm.

The goal of this format is to have everything viewable in six visual degrees, so your eyes can move down but not require horizontal movement like normal books.

This increase reading speed and accuracy.

Unfortunately, not all publishers or devices allow this format.

Editors include Mom, Kathy Gerhardt, Roan Kirschbaum, Will Bradley, Doug Kalagian, Matt Drees, Afsah Hussain, and Bri Dorgan.

Ideas for artwork from Angrra
Mitha, Alex Pickles Nichols, Matt
Nelson, Michelle Bell.

Thanks to the following for ideas
or concepts: Mom, Dad, Dillon,
Amiya, Kathy, Drees, Afsah,
William, Doug, Leo, Mitha, Beny,
Whomod, Adam, Alex, Todd,
Ricky, Jake, Scott, Aaron,
Roanus-King, Jim, Ellen, Enee,
Nora, Stacy, Zorro, Potatoman,
Rengo, Parker, Joel, Ben, Bri,
Kallan, Annie, Emily, Casey,
Nick, Jason, Sam, Kim, Jolie,
Ben, Dave, Sena, Mitzi,
Grandma, and Grandpa, Ray,
Jet, Andi, Jessica, Harsh, AJ,
Brig, Zak, Don, Michelle, Matt,
Tony, Carl, David, Jacob, Tim,
Brian, Kevin, Devin, Miles, Seth,
Seiji, Nan, Earl, Joanne, Deanna,
Melissa, Jarmo, Luke, Kaz, Icy,
Erica, Joey, Gilb, Peter, Robin,
Meg, Nan, Malorie, Soleil, Aimee,
Patty, George, Gireesh, Katina,
Logan, Matt, Sonya, Sena, Mitzi,
N, Dana, Nam, Amer, Armstrong,

Michael, Eric, Daniel, Arthur, Jan, Steve, Pickles, Tate, and Bucky.

If you want to chat, then message 42cherrytrees at gmail dot com.

Warning responses may be delayed because some years unable to access my email.

REFERENCES

[i] Rosling, H. (2016). *Numbers are boring, people are interesting.* Retrieved 2018, from https://www.youtube.com/watch?v=nh94kK05l-M

[ii] Scorse, J. (2012). *Environmental and Natural Resource Economics.* Middlebury Institute of International Studies.

[iii] Roser, M. (n.d.). *War and Peace.* Our World in Data. Retrieved 2018, from https://ourworldindata.org/war-and-peace

[iv] Dalio, R. (2017). *Our Biggest Economic, Social, and Political Issue.* LinkedIn. Retrieved 2018, from https://www.linkedin.com/pulse/our-biggest-economic-social-political-issue-two-economies-ray-dalio

[v] Thiel, P. (2014). *Zero to One: Notes on Startups, or How to Build the Future.* Crown Business. New York. Retrieved 2018, from https://www.amazon.com/Zero-One-Notes-Startups-Future/dp/0804139296

[vi] Shmoop Editorial Team. (2008, November 11). *The Great Depression Statistics.* Retrieved June 5, 2018, from https://www.shmoop.com/great-depression/statistics.html

[vii] Dalio, R., & Blodgett, H. (2017). *RAY DALIO: You have to bet against the consensus and be right to be successful in the markets. Business Insider.* Retrieved 2018, from http://www.businessinsider.com/ray-dalio-bridgewater-breaks-down-fundamental-investment-approach-2017-9

[viii] Kemp, J. (2014). *Jeff Kemp Lessons.* Retrieved 2018, from http://www.jeffkemplessons.com/

[ix] Dalio, R. (2013). *How The Economic Machine Works.* Retrieved 2018, from https://youtu.be/PHe0bXAIuk0

[x] Ziemba, W. (2018). *Initial public offering - Alpha Z Advisors.* Retrieved 2018, from http://alphazadvisors.com/initial-public-offering/

[xi] Taleb, N. (2010). *The Black Swan: Second Edition: The Impact of the Highly Improbable.* Random House. New York. Retrieved 2018, from https://www.amazon.com/Black-Swan-Second-Improbable-Incerto-ebook/dp/B00139XTG4

[xii] O'Shaughnessy, P. (2014). *Millennial Money: How Young Investors Can Build a Fortune.* Palgrave Macmillan. New York. Retrieved 2018, from https://www.amazon.com/Millennial-Money-Young-Investors-Fortune-ebook/dp/B00JTIU1QM

[xiii] Rowland, C., & Lawson, J. M. (2012). The Permanent Portfolio: Harry Browne's Long-Term Investment Strategy. Retrieved 2018, from https://www.amazon.com/Permanent-Portfolio-Long-Term-Investment-Strategy/dp/1118288254

[xiv] Dalio, R., & Robbins, T. (2018). *The End of the Bull Market - Team Tony.* Retrieved 2018, from https://www.tonyrobbins.com/wealth-lifestyle/the-end-of-the-bull-market/

[xv] Carlson, B. (2014*). Back-Testing The Tony Robbins All-Weather Portfolio - A Wealth of Common Sense.* Retrieved 2018, from

http://awealthofcommonsense.com/2014/11/back-testing-tony-robbins-weather-portfolio/

xvi Rohrbaugh, E. (2015). *Duplicating The All-Weather Fund Using Low-Cost ETFs – Seeking Alpha*. Retrieved 2018, from https://seekingalpha.com/article/3350735-duplicating-the-all-weather-fund-using-low-cost-etfs

xvii Portfolio Visualizer. (2018). *Backtest Portfolio Asset Allocation*. Retrieved 2018, from https://www.portfoliovisualizer.com/backtest-asset-class-allocation

xviii (2018). *Member States | United Nations - UN.org*. Retrieved 2018, from http://www.un.org/en/member-states/

xix (2017). *Giving USA 2017: Total Charitable Donations Rise to New High of $390.05 Billion*. Retrieved 2018, from https://givingusa.org/giving-usa-2017-total-charitable-donations-rise-to-new-high-of-390-05-billion/

xx Thorp, E. O. (2017). *A Man for All Markets: From Las Vegas to Wall Street, How I Beat the Dealer and the Market*. Random House. New York. Retrieved 2018, from https://www.amazon.com/Man-All-Markets-Street-Dealer-ebook/dp/B00SEFEYCI

xxi Rosling, H. (2014). *DON'T PANIC*. Gapminder Foundation. Retrieved 2018, from http://www.youtube.com/oembed?format=xml&url=https://www.youtube.com/watch?v=FACK2knC08E&list=FLdUmWkN1OJ5raySHeVrnkxw&index=17

xxii (2017). COUNTRY COMPARISON :: TOTAL FERTILITY RATE. CIA World Factbook. Retrieved 2018, from https://www.cia.gov/library/publications/the-world-factbook/rankorder/2127rank.html

xxiii UC Davis Center for Poverty. (2017) *What are the poverty thresholds today?* Retrieved 2018, from http://poverty.ucdavis.edu/faq/what-are-poverty-thresholds-today.

xxiv McGonigal, K. (2013). *How Self-Control Works, Why It Matters, and What You Can Do to Get More of It*. Penguin Group. New York. Retrieved 2018, from https://www.amazon.com/Willpower-Instinct-Self-Control-Works-Matters/dp/1583335080

xxv Dalio, R. (2017). *Principles: Life and Work*. Simon & Schuster. New York. Retrieved 2018, from https://www.amazon.com/Principles-Life-Work-Ray-Dalio-ebook/dp/B071CTK28D/ref=tmm_kin_swatch_0?_encoding=UTF8&qid=&sr=

xxvi Dalio, R. (2018). *Principles for Success - An Ultra Mini Series Adventure*. Retrieved 2018, from https://www.principles.com/principles-for-success/

xxvii Taleb, N. (2010). *The Black Swan: Second Edition: The Impact of the Highly Improbable*. Retrieved 2018, from https://www.amazon.com/Black-Swan-Improbable-Robustness-Fragility/dp/081297381X

www.ingramcontent.com/pod-product-compliance
Lightning Source LLC
Chambersburg PA
CBHW022050190326
41520CB00008B/762